HOME SERIES

HOME SERIES
LIVING ROOMS

BETA-PLUS

CONTENTS

8   Foreword

14   Art Deco accents in Milan
20   The metamorphosis of a historic house
24   Pure sophistication in a French-inspired manor
28   The renovation of a city home
38   The sympathetic restoration of an old presbytery
42   A refuge for a pair of antiques dealers
48   A dynamic country house
52   The cosy interior of a country house
60   A sober and sophisticated living environment
64   An avant-garde spirit
68   A view of the Thames
72   A new transparency
76   A tasteful combination
82   The restoration of a 17th-century abbey farmhouse
88   Serenity and refinement in a cosmopolitan atmosphere
92   The metamorphosis of a Directoire house
98   The restoration of an authentic mansion
102   A passion for the 1930s
106   A symbiosis of contrasts
110   A sense of detail
114   A duplex apartment in a former school
120   Moroccan nuances in a holiday home

P. 4-5
Axel Pairon took his inspiration
from modernity and saturated
colours when furnishing this
seaside apartment.

P. 6
Vlassak-Verhulst's reception lounge.
A mahogany coffee table and a gas
fire in split slate.
Silk carpet.

FOREWORD

T he living room is one of the most important spaces in the house, for rest, relaxation, entertainment, family gatherings, welcoming visitors, hobbies, and many other purposes.

This room is the real heart of the house, a transitional space between the outside world and the more private areas of the home, such as bedrooms and bathrooms. When it comes to furnishing and decoration, the living room is traditionally the space that receives most attention – and rightly so. This is the place in the home where we usually spend most of our time and the first room that guests see.

The sitting room and living room reflect the taste of the owners and their lifestyle – and often even their philosophy of life – but these are also social places, where people get together. The colours, materials and the style of furniture are all indications of the owners' tastes and expectations.

Times and tastes change. Nowadays, it is unusual to find two separate living areas in a home: a sitting room for formal occasions and a smaller living room for everyday life.

The multifunctional character of the modern living room creates certain difficulties. The aim is to make a space that satisfies all of the many different requirements, which means that furnishing the room efficiently and harmoniously is not an easy task.

The projects in this book reflect current trends and fashions and feature a diversity of styles: rustic and ultramodern, brightly coloured and in natural shades. The intention is not to present rigid codes for decoration, but instead to give everyone the opportunity to leaf through the pages and be inspired by the wide variety of interiors.

P. 8
An interior by B. Lecot.
Harmony between the curtains
and the colour of the walls.

P. 10-11
A stone floor in Bleu de Vix
(50x70 cm) in a home designed
by architect Bernard De Clerck.

ART DECO ACCENTS

IN MILAN

This Art Deco-inspired apartment in the centre of Milan is situated on the top floor of a building from 1911.

The designer Romeo Sozzi, owner of Promemoria (contemporary Italian furniture), spent two years on this project, a gallery for his art collection, with the most exclusive of pieces displayed in an oasis of calm and serenity.

The unusual colour that predominates in this room is a muted one, close to the colour of walnuts. The result is a sophisticated and cosy look.

Particular attention has been devoted to the choice of materials: Sozzi's project ingeniously integrates velvet, silk, crocodile skin and mahogany.
These elements evoke a genuine Art Deco atmosphere.
Balance in the room, between light and dark, functionality and emotion – this is Promemoria's philosophy.

A mahogany Simon daybed in ivory velvet. Candelabro candle unit with mirror behind. An Agatha table lamp.

A Wanda sofa in old beech wood and viscose velour.
A beautiful Kingwood cupboard in morado with bronze handles.

P. 16-17
A *bergère* beech armchair, in a woven blue fabric, with a Dafne lamp behind. A Françoise table lamp on the Hugo mahogany desk with interior in maple and bronze details. Brigitta Short chair in old beech wood upholstered in cream hammered leather.

P. 18-19
A Bellagio sofa in mahogany and linen, a Club armchair, an Oolong sideboard and an Arthur footstool. In the centre, a Sapphire bench in mahogany.

THE METAMORPHOSIS

OF A HISTORIC HOUSE

S ources say that this country house was built in 1657 on a large estate for a noble family. After a complete transformation over the course of the centuries, this unique property was acquired by the exclusive construction company Vlassak-Verhulst.

This historic residence now has a very contemporary atmosphere: sober forms and colours in an elegant and streamlined sitting room. The strengths of this interior are in the symmetrical positioning of the furniture and the use of a timeless colour palette (black, white, grey), accentuated by a number of deep-red touches.

The oak floor has a naturally aged finish. An antique fireplace in Belgian red marble with a gas fire. The walls have a white lime finish. Lamps with bronze base and shades in natural silk. Black leather armchairs with a mahogany frame and suede cushions.

A nod to the art of antiquity with plaster mouldings, inspired by Ionic columns.

P. 22-23
An oak fireplace, with a gas fire, finished in white plaster.
Silk armchairs, a coffee table in grey bamboo and two mahogany
occasional tables.
Lamps in grey crystal with a silk shade. Parquet in Hungarian point.

PURE SOPHISTICATION

IN A FRENCH-INSPIRED MANOR

C ostermans constructed this French-inspired manor, situated in magnificent natural surroundings, in a warm, classic style.

The greatest of care was taken over the selection of materials, including unusual old tiles and floors, historical wooden boards and unique fireplaces.

The whole project has a timeless character. Classicism, brought up to date with a few daring touches: a Louis XIII-style armchair is upholstered in an apple-green fabric, an Eames lounge chair harmonises with a rustic chair. This classic home is full of surprising elements that give it a contemporary touch.

An old French oak floor, in Hungarian point.

In the sitting room, a French Louis XI fireplace beside a Louis XIII-style chair, upholstered in an apple-green fabric.

A bold, but successful combination of antique and contemporary furniture (lounge chair and Ottoman by Vitra Classic, designed by Charles and Ray Eames) in this TV room.

THE RENOVATION

OF A CITY HOME

A family with four older children commissioned architect Baudouin Courtens to change some of the interior elements in their new city home.

The result: a comfortable home that is full of light, a custom-made sanctuary that reflects the owners' dynamic and modern lifestyle.

The living room is streamlined and geometric. The dining room also has clean lines, but the blond wood gives it a warmer feel.

All of the walls on the ground floor were demolished to create a new open space with a kitchen and dining room and a wonderful view of the garden.
The living room extends over the entire breadth of the house on the side facing the garden.
The structure of horizontal lines in the fireplace and the sofas give this house a serene atmosphere.

P. 29-33
Subtle simplicity: the owners' beautiful collection of contemporary art and a few well-chosen pieces of furniture. These elements determined the choice of materials and colours.

The designer restricted the colour palette to reinforce the sense of harmony.

THE SYMPATHETIC RESTORATION

OF AN OLD PRESBYTERY

T he owners of this old presbytery from 1765 have had it meticulously restored.

Interior architect Nathalie Van Reeth created a timeless look in perfect harmony with the historic surroundings. The use of a sober, sophisticated range of muted colours for the fabrics and floors (greige, grey, taupe) has created a restful atmosphere.

The department for the preservation of historic buildings insisted that the existing mouldings and mantelpiece should remain intact.
The large, custom-made sofa is upholstered in velvet. The natural linen carpet was made specially for this living room.

Axel and Boris Vervoordt selected the custom-made shelving, the mirror, the lamp and the coffee table.
Silk curtains.

Calming shades of grey for the walls and the grey linen sofa in this TV room. The old mouldings have been restored; the mantelpiece is a recent addition.

A REFUGE FOR A PAIR

OF ANTIQUES DEALERS

Alain and Brigitte Garnier, a married couple of antiques dealers, purchased the historic estate of Vaucelle in 1999. Some elements of the abbey and farmhouse from the 17th, 18th and 19th centuries remain intact.

The restoration work took over eight years.

The result was a cosy interior that respects the historic character of the estate.

The period furniture guarantees sophistication and authenticity.

Garnier created the large, custom-made sofa in celadon linen. The eighteenth-century fireplace is in Burgundy imitation marble.
Curtains in taffeta silk. Hillite lighting. Antique chairs from the seventeenth and eighteenth centuries and an antique parquet floor, in Hungarian point.
The coffee table has a surface in old laminated elm wood with a wrought-iron frame.

P. 44-45
Two Louis XIV chairs.

A wine table and a small Swedish table
(18th century) beside a 360cm sofa,
made by Garnier.
The square painting is by Tiepolo.

A painting by Faustino Bocchi
(1659–1742) on the wooden
mantelpiece. The seventeenth-century
elm floor was found in Lille.

Custom-made panelling (both old and new) is one of Garnier's specialities.

A DYNAMIC COUNTRY HOUSE

P op colours in this contemporary country house. Designer Gert Voorjans took an eclectic approach to this interior: a surprising mix of old and modern elements in a setting with bright and vivid colours.

This refreshing and unexpected cocktail creates a lively, dynamic atmosphere in this classic house.

A good tip from this report: revitalising rustic furniture with upholstery in trendy fabrics and colours. This is an imaginative touch, tempered by the pale walls.

An English wing chair and an armchair upholstered in a Tuscan fabric beside a library table.

This shelving unit separates the dining room from the living room.

P. 50-51
An eye-catching feature in the centre of the
living room: a Biedermeier chair.

THE COSY INTERIOR

OF A COUNTRY HOUSE

T his country house, recently built by architect Van Vlierberghe, was furnished by the Descamps interior consultancy, Garnier antiques and La Campagne.

They succeeded in the challenge: this new house has all the charm of days gone by. This is an absolute *tour de force*, supported by the use of period furniture, patinated walls and old construction materials.

The sofa (model: Poly) was custom-made by Garnier, as was the coffee table with an old elm surface and wrought-iron base.

The table, lamp and painting are from La Campagne. Garnier selected the eighteenth-century carpet.

Two walnut-wood armchairs around a table, also in walnut wood, from Germany.

An old wine table, an *os de mouton* chair and, in the background, a Louis XIII armchair.

The oak panels date from the 18th century and are from Holland. Garnier gave them a new finish. Garnier custom-made the round dining table with a central leg in the company's own workshop. Ten 19th-century chairs and, left, a walnut-wood console with an original surface in red marble.

La Campagne found this banquette.

The dining room is directly connected to the kitchen. Antiques from Garnier and La Campagne.

A SOBER AND SOPHISTICATED

LIVING ENVIRONMENT

This spacious apartment has been transformed into a holiday home for a family with young children. The consultancy Sphere/Sphere Projects created this interior in a quest for pure, sober forms and a subtle colour palette. The result is a restful home that is bathed in the colours of the North Sea: sand, greige, and grey.

Nothing disturbs the clean lines of this interior: an interplay of pale and blond shades for the walls and furniture.

A subtle mixture of old and new in this calm atmosphere: some beautiful old objects from distant cultures, a contemporary painting, an untreated oak floor, natural linen and an almost monochrome colour palette.

The custom-made unit beneath the plasma screen is in aged oak.
A coffee table with an oak surface and a wrought-iron base.

All of the furniture and objects are from Sphere.

AN AVANT-GARDE SPIRIT

E nsemble & Associés interior-design consultancy designed this apartment of over 300 m^2.

Light, space, perspective: a magic formula with a combination of luxury materials in a streamlined setting. This custom-made interior gives this exclusive space a very special atmosphere.

A real lesson in simplicity in this minimalist interior, which is based on a careful selection of luxury materials.

P. 64-67
The parquet floor in grey-tinted oak has a matte varnish finish. A corner gas fireplace, designed and created for this space. Custom-made coffee tables in tinted oak and bronze. Armchairs by Minotti and a Flexform sofa.
In the background, p. 67: Knoll chairs around a long table (320x150 cm), specially designed in tinted oak with a gleaming chrome finish. Glossy, self-supporting surfaces.

A VIEW OF THE THAMES

G illes de Meulemeester redesigned this pied-à-terre, situated by the Thames in a building by Richard Rogers. His mission: to create a comfortable living environment that was full of light.

The brief involved orienting the space to take best advantage of the beautiful views over London. The living room is chic and contemporary with its bronze and dark woods and fabric. The dining room, which is warmer and lighter, is in paler varieties of wood and cream leather, with an echo of the dark wood in the mirror frame. This extends the view of the Thames and the length of the living room.

The furniture is from the Promemoria and Interni collections.

A Bristol table, sideboard, armchairs and Caffè large chairs. A Reflets mirror, a Milleraies carpet and a Move lamp.

P. 70-71
Beau Rivage sofas, Loren armchairs and a Manhattan padded table beneath a work by artist Christine Nicaise.

A NEW TRANSPARENCY

When architect Baudouin Courtens was asked to make a few changes to the interior of a country house, he realised that the division of the space in the house no longer satisfied the owners' modern way of life and that the beautiful garden had not been integrated into the interior.

So he suggested that his clients should have the ground floor completely redesigned and add a new extension with a large living room.

The continuity between the interior and the exterior is further reinforced by the use of the same floor throughout the living room and on the terraces (bluestone, with an Agrippa finish).

Luxury materials (bluestone, oak, lime paints, linen and leather) in a limited palette of colours in the living room – extending this approach to the other living areas has created a strong sense of harmony.

The sober, serene atmosphere is the perfect environment for the owners' art collection.

Kitchen, dining room, wine cellar and reception room follow on from each other in this space divided by sliding doors.

A TASTEFUL COMBINATION

T he sumptuous facade of this neo-classical house from the early eighteenth century conceals a beautiful apartment that was recently restored by architect Olivier Dwek, in collaboration with Robert De Groeve.

They were commissioned by a married couple who are keen art collectors and passionate about the modern art of the twentieth century.

This project shows a tasteful combination of pure forms and volumes, which is typical of Dwek's work, combined with the unique atmosphere created by De Groeve.

Le Crin blinds and Jim Thompson curtains in linen and silk.
A JNL daybed upholstered in silk and linen.

Olivier Dwek created this shelving unit as a monumental and pure object, with depth and proportions playing a central role.

P. 78-79
A coffee table designed by Ado Chale and
built in Brazilian agate. Lamps and sofas by
JNL, art by C. Lalanne, F. Léger, J. Deyrolle
and G. Segal.

THE RESTORATION OF

A 17TH-CENTURY ABBEY FARMHOUSE

Architect Bernard De Clerck completely restored the main building, stables, barn, gatehouse and service quarters of this abbey farmhouse, which dates back to the seventeenth century.

The result was a light and airy farmhouse, in a contemporary classic design, devoid of references to the traditional rustic furnishings of such farmhouses.

The materials, including bleached wood, beams in untreated wood and linen curtains, further reinforce the serenity and calming character of this home.

Garnier supplied the antique objects; the old building materials are from Rik Storms.

The floor in the summer sitting room is in old terracotta tiles.

The interplay of light creates a cosy atmosphere in this summer room.

P. 84 and above
The walls in the daytime living room are in bleached elm panels.
The windows look out over the mezzanine. Beneath this is the entrance to the old vaulted cellar.

Painted wooden panelling throughout the library.

P. 86-87
The stone of the chimney has been painted black.

SERENITY AND REFINEMENT

IN A COSMOPOLITAN ATMOSPHERE

A big-city, cosmopolitan atmosphere in green surroundings on the outskirts of Brussels, but still close to the city centre: this private residence, created by architect Marc Corbiau, offers the best of both worlds.

Raoul Cavadias, a Belgian designer with Greek roots, who was born in Africa and grew up in Switzerland, created the interior design of this distinctive city villa, with its atmosphere of space, serenity and sophistication.
Discreet luxury in the selection of materials and dark wood in this contemporary interior with a definite masculine feel.

Coffee tables in treated zinc designed by Raoul Cavadias. Sisal carpet.

A low sideboard unit separates the dining room from the living room. Blinds in dark teakwood.

The panelling in the TV room is in bleached teakwood. The coffee table is a design by Christian Liaigre; the window seat in woven leather is a creation by Raoul Cavadias.

The table in the dining room is a creation by Vincent Van Duysen, with twisted legs in solid beech and a slate surface. Chairs by Christian Liaigre.

THE METAMORPHOSIS

OF A DIRECTOIRE HOUSE

A rchitect Bernard De Clerck lived for over a decade in a Directoire house, which dates back to the early nineteenth century.

The house was restored with respect for the features of the Directoire style: simplicity, light and spacious volumes and an absence of superfluous ornamentation.

The rooms are linked together in intriguing arrangements that offer beautiful views through the house.

De Clerck added an orangery and restored the original character of some of the windows. The shutters are used mainly in the summer to filter the sunlight.

The tall windows connect the sitting room and the sun terrace.

Oil paintings with faded colours.

The small sitting room at the front of the house. Some of the wide doors of this house have been replaced by double doors. This room has a Tuscan feel, which complements the Directoire style.

In the summer, the only plant sheltering in the winter garden is the stump of a very old araucaria from the garden. This room provides access to the master bedroom: the winter garden is one of the best places to study in this house, early in the morning or late at night.

Upstairs, shades of pale grey and white combine with old, honey-coloured pitchpine floors to create a restful atmosphere.

This upstairs room with an open fireplace is a winter sitting room, with a touch of nostalgia for the Far East.

THE RESTORATION

OF AN AUTHENTIC MANSION

This grand house, dating back to 1880, has been thoroughly restored by J. Reynders and interior designer Helena van den Driessche, in close collaboration with the owners.

During the restoration works, they made good use of the special features of the house (the very high ceilings, tall doors and windows, balanced structure and layout of the rooms) in order to safeguard the unique cachet of this distinctive property.

The typical elements of a nineteenth-century mansion have remained intact: the high ceilings, the tall windows and doors. These features open up the space, allowing in the perfect amount of light.
Other authentic elements, such as mouldings, glass doors and fireplaces, have also been retained.

To gain maximum benefit from the light, there are no curtains. A custom-made table lamp by Histoire de Famille (Fabienne Verbesselt).

They added a glass door (behind the large sofa on the left in the photograph) to allow more light into the narrow stairway, which is a typical feature of this kind of house.

A PASSION FOR THE 1930S

T his 1926 *bel-étage* house was designed by architect Herman Van Ooteghem and is in an area that is known for its eclectic architecture, ranging from neo-classicism to the pure design of the Bauhaus.

This house is an almost square construction with two floors. The stairway with its strange, yet elegant forms is an eye-catching feature that reveals the 1930s origins of the house.

Interior architect Vanessa De Meulder completely redesigned the living areas, with respect for the original elements and proportions.

P. 102-105

White is present throughout this home, with a few dark touches as a contrast.

Vanessa De Meulder designed the sofas and the coffee tables in brushed stainless steel. The bright and colourful African theme breaks up the interplay of black and white.

Silver pieces by Annick Tapernoux.

A lamp by Eileen Grey. A Limited Edition carpet in harmony with the colour of the parquet floor.

A SYMBIOSIS OF CONTRASTS

S ober yet sophisticated, geometric but warm and cosy: these are just some of the many contrasts with which interior architect Philip Simoen plays in all of his projects.

This interior is a fine illustration of this symbiosis of contrasts.

P. 106 and 108-109
GroundPiece sofas by Flexform around a B&B Italia coffee table designed by Antonio Citterio. A Carpet Sign rug, Moooi lamp (Marcel Wanders) and Linara curtains (Romo). Art by Sol LeWitt.

Table and chairs were designed by Citterio for Maxalto. The wall-mounted cupboard unit is a creation by Philip Simoen. In the background, a bowl by John Pawson.

A SENSE OF DETAIL

T his duplex apartment is a project by interior architect Stavit Mor in collaboration with Obumex. The home has a very serene and calming atmosphere. The interior architect has aimed to create a smooth integration of all of the rooms within the larger whole; her sophistication and sense of detail is a theme that runs through the whole project.

This apartment is on the coast, but is used all year round, not only in the summer.
The designer selected pastel shades and warm colours, complemented by a few dark touches.

Openness is central to this duplex apartment: every room flows seamlessly into the next.

Obumex created the sideboard, a design by Stavit Mor.
Promemoria chairs around a dining table by Christian Liaigre.

Central in the background, a work by Christine Nicaise. Poufs in embroidered leather around a wooden coffee table. The linen carpet creates a warm look. Parquet in aged oak.

P. 112-113
A Promemoria console in wood and leather serves as a radiator box.

A DUPLEX APARTMENT

IN A FORMER SCHOOL

This former school, perfectly situated on one of Amsterdam's most beautiful canals, has been transformed into a complex of eleven apartments.

Dutch interior architect Marijke van Nunen was entrusted with the delicate task of completely furnishing one of these apartments. As the space was empty and unfinished, Van Nunen was able to specify all of the details: the layout and size of the rooms, the choice of materials for the floors, walls and ceilings, the stairs, the kitchen and the bathrooms, right down to the doors and fittings.

This apartment consists of two floors with a mezzanine for the library. Both levels have a view of the canals.
The oversized decorative elements add drama to the apartment, demonstrating the interior architect's bold approach to volume and giving this home a unique character.

All of the walls are plastered and painted. The plant decorations are by Paul Klunder.

A view of the living room (ceiling with a height of 4.75 m), as seen from the dining room. The curtain rails are in solid iron, and the curtains themselves are in acetate. The furniture is upholstered with a thick linen fabric.

The windows (three large and two small) have a panoramic view of Amsterdam's canals. The cushions on the radiator boxes allow them to be used as a seat.

The area around the fireplace has a view of the mezzanine on one side and the canal on the other.

On the mezzanine, Marijke van Nunen decided to install a wooden floor in untreated oak. The space has a low beamed ceiling and custom-made shelf units.
The *chaises longues* and the pouf are in a thick linen. The mezzanine has a view of the living room.

The walls of the stairway have a plaster finish; the steps are in untreated oak.

P. 118-119
Perfect harmony between the large sofa (also in a thick linen) and the coffee table and matching bench, made from long planks. A thick Abaca carpet.

MOROCCAN NUANCES

IN A HOLIDAY HOME

Interior designer Brigitte Peten furnished this small house in wooded surroundings.

The owners have a passion for Morocco, as their house reveals, with its typically Moroccan style, right down to the colour palette: terracotta, paprika, taupe and caramel.

The parquet floor is in aged oak. The house is suffused with an atmosphere of calm and warmth.

The TV room with a sofa-bed from Marie's Corner in linen. Cushions by Ralph Lauren. Silk curtains lined with a thick striped fabric, Ticka by Malabar. The English occasional table (19th century) is from Garnier, as are the lamp and the collection of Chinese Han vases.

The dining room is warm and inviting.
The 18th-century Italian table is in walnut wood. Two 17th-century os de mouton armchairs upholstered in a fabric by Malabar.
The new chairs, also os de mouton, are in Bartu fabrics. An antique pot has been transformed into a lamp.

P. 122-123
The work of art on the left of the photograph is by
Christine Morin.
Garnier created the oak coffee table with a surface
in Portuguese marble. The decorative objects on
the left of the fireplace (fish teeth) are by Garnier.

HOME SERIES

Volume 1: LIVING ROOMS

The reports in this book are selected from the Beta-Plus collection of home-design books: www.betaplus.com
They have been compiled in a special series by Le Figaro in French language: Ma Déco

Copyright © 2009 Beta-Plus Publishing / Le Figaro
Originally published in French language

PUBLISHER
Beta-Plus Publishing
Termuninck 3
B – 7850 Enghien
Belgium
www.betaplus.com
info@betaplus.com

PHOTOGRAPHY
Jo Pauwels

DESIGN
Polydem - Nathalie Binart

TRANSLATIONS
Laura Watkinson

ISBN: 9789089440327

Printed in China

P. 126-127
A project by Themenos.